HOLY GOD, HOLY PEOPLE

by Mike O'Neal

1ˢᵗ THESS. 4:8 - GOD GIVES ↑

1ˢᵗ COR. 3:16-17-GOD's SPIRIT

EPH. 2:22 - YOU ARE BEING BUIL
FOR GOD BY the SPIRIT

2ᴺᴰ COR. 6:16 - WE ARE the TEMPLE of the LIVING GOD

COL. 3:11 - CHRIST IS ALL & IS IN ALL

JOHN 16:7 -

JER. 31:31-34 ~

2 COR. 3:3-8

21ˢᵗ CENTURY CHRISTIAN

ISBN: 978-0-89098-583-0
eISBN: 978-0-89098-983-8

©2012 by 21st Century Christian
2809 12th Ave S., Nashville, TN 37204

Cover design by Jonathan Edelhuber

Jim Wright
706-633-7007

Table of Contents

Introduction

We've been told that *"Image is everything." "Take good care of what shows and don't worry about the rest."* God's agenda for our lives, however, is much different. He wants to change us from the inside out. The "image" that has been tarnished by sin can only be restored by the power of God.

God displays His infinite holiness through Scripture. He longs to transform us into His holy people and uses His holy angels, the Holy Spirit, and sanctified Christians to accomplish His purposes. A holy God invites you into the lifelong journey to become His holy people.

About the Author

Mike O'Neal is a graduate of Harding School of Theology and has served as minister for several congregations in central Florida. He is now a retired NASA engineer after 31 years of service at the Kennedy Space Center. While there, he worked on Space Shuttle missions and investigated ways to provide spiritual support for astronauts on long-duration missions. Mike is also the author of *An Angel's View* **(21st Century Christian Publishing)**. He speaks frequently about angels, spirituality, and spaceflight.

Lesson 1
Why Study About Holiness?

Daily Readings:
Hebrews 12:14; Leviticus 11:44-45, 19:2; 1 Peter 1:15-16; John 1:18, 14:9-11; Isaiah 6:1-5; Philippians 3:17-19; Luke 5:8

WARM UP

About half-way through my degree program at the Harding University Graduate School of Religion, my coursework started to become a bit of a grind. With all my electives gone, only core courses remained. Most of these required classes were fairly interesting, but I typically enjoyed the electives much better. Drawn to their subject matter, they were courses of my choosing, not some mind-numbing class required by the school.

One day, while looking at my remaining classes, I noticed Restoration Church History was still on the horizon, when suddenly a great idea hit me. It was time to grovel at the feet of the Dean and ask for a waiver. Just turning forty-eight years old and chomping at the bit to do ministry, the only history I wanted to study was in the Bible, so taking an extra class on one of its books was my goal. Graciously, though directly, the Dean explained the importance of understanding the roots of our faith-heritage and turned down my feeble attempt at a waiver. His point-of-view was dead-on, but I still dreaded taking this class. Despite my reservations, Restoration Church History turned out to be one of my all-time favorites. The incredible devotion and achievements by those who had gone before me was truly inspirational. From my new vantage point, several additional heroes of faith were added to my list of those from God's Word.

For all Christians, studying the topic of holiness should be considered a core requirement, never to be waived. As we passionately explore this important subject together, hopefully your newly-gained vantage point will bring new life and understanding to your Christian walk.

WORK OUT

You are not alone if the concept of holiness is a little gray to you. In our culture, the term is rarely used in secular settings, and when it is, the tone tends to be derogatory. You might recall such phrases as "You think you are holier than everyone else," or "They are just a bunch of holy rollers." Even in our churches, you hardly ever hear a sermon on holiness or have an in-depth class on the subject.

Scripture uses it in different ways. Sometimes holiness carries an ethical meaning, while at other times it denotes something's unique nature, and in a few cases both dimensions may be implied. So context will always need to be evaluated to determine what is appropriate. To make matters worse, the words related to holiness, such as "sanctify" and "saint," carry with them their own confusing aspects.

Consequently, we have an interesting challenge in front of us, but as we peel back this onion, things will become a lot clearer. For now, let's look at a couple of important reasons for studying this crucial topic.

Heavenly Prerequisite

Many of our desires in life necessitate completing prerequisites before proceeding on to our true objectives. This usually involves obtaining some level of proficiency in the activity being pursued. For example, our highways are scary enough. Could you imagine how dangerous they would be if no evaluation of a person's driving skills occurred prior to issuing them a license?

The author of Hebrews reveals a sobering prerequisite for the Christian – "without which no one will see the Lord" (Hebrews 12:14). Holiness is not some optional extra; it is standard equipment for God's people. To stand in the presence of our holy God, those who profess His name must possess holiness. Therefore, believers are told to pursue this invaluable characteristic. So what is it that we are actually pursuing? With such a weighty end-result in view, obtaining the proper understanding of the concept of holiness is crucial. As you will see, our gracious God does not make such a lofty demand and leave us to our own meager resources, but He facilitates the development of holiness within His people.

Be Like Whom?

If you are like me, most of you have looked up to a role model or two throughout the years. However, you probably learned fairly quickly that living up to the standards and performance of those we admire can be a tall order. Knowing this to be the case, Scripture again appears to place the Christian in a tough predicament. When it comes to holiness, we must follow in God's footsteps. Both the Old and New

Testaments make it perfectly clear that God's people are to emulate His holy ways (Leviticus 11:44-45, 19:2; 1 Peter 1:15-16). To be like God in any particular way sounds daunting enough, but when combined with holiness's abstract nature, a white cloud may pop up above our head with the thought, "You want me to do what!?"

Perhaps now you understand why a course on holiness should be a core requirement for God's people. Since so much is at stake, we need to properly ground ourselves in this important subject. Within God's Word we will find ample information to understand the concept of holiness, so "hang in there." Scripture thoroughly attests to God's holiness, and we must always remember that Jesus is the great revealer of His Father (John 1:18, 14:9-11). Holiness radiated throughout and defined Jesus' earthly ministry.

COOL DOWN

Early in my career at NASA, I worked on the Space Shuttle Main Engine Avionics Subsystem. This consisted of the computers, electronics, and instrumentation that controlled the three Main Engines, which each delivered 375,000 pounds of thrust to the Shuttle at liftoff. Honeywell designed and built the avionics box that controlled these high-energy beasts. One of the greatest privileges of my career was working with the Honeywell designers. No doubt, when it came to electronics design, they were some of our nation's elite. I loved rubbing elbows with them at design reviews, but at times I felt intimidated due to their utter brilliance and professionalism. Not that they did anything to intentionally create such a reaction; my own inadequacies just seemed to internally come to light while in the company of these phenomenal engineers.

Isaiah would probably empathize with such feelings, though in a much more significant way. When he encountered God in his throne room vision, a horrible dread immediately swept over him (Isaiah 6:5). His sinful condition at once came into view as He stood in the presence of the All-Holy One. Peter also had a similar response to Jesus after the miraculous catch of fish (Luke 5:8).

At the early stages of your Christianity, you probably also felt a similar discomfort when spending time with individuals you deemed as holy. As you observed their impeccable lifestyle, the thought of your own weaknesses and vices most likely created feelings of inadequacy within you. Regrettably, in such circumstances, uneasiness overtakes us, and we may even tend to avoid this person. Most of us seek ways to escape discomfort and reminders of our inadequacies.

Although such reactions are inevitable, consider the following. First, we desperately need role models in our lives that exemplify holiness. Paul appealed to the Philippians to find godly examples to follow (Philippians 3:17). Holiness is not an option; it must be pursued and finding good role models places us on the right track.

Second, those who consider themselves as potential role models need to go the extra mile in becoming approachable. Let your holy behavior be observed outside the "sanctity" of the church building in neutral settings. Share your hobbies, go fishing, play softball, discuss home projects, or whatever "floats your boat." Just create some experiences in which others can relate to you as a person - take the scary out of holy.

Third, if you truly desire to pursue holiness, any discomfort you might experience from being around someone who exhibits a holy lifestyle will probably be fleeting. You will discover that they are not free of weaknesses and that they rely upon God for their holiness. Pray for courage and step into a relationship that will have eternal ramifications. Finally, Jesus invites you to view His life – the ideal holy life.

Questions

1. When you hear or read the word "holy," what typically comes to mind?
2. Do you view yourself as a holy person? Why or why not?
3. Do you think studying about holiness is important? Explain.
4. What do you think of the requirement to be holy like God? Do you think that is achievable?
5. Have you ever felt uncomfortable in the presence of someone you viewed as holy? What created your discomfort? What might help overcome this discomfort?
6. Do you believe having holy role models is important? What would you expect out of such a relationship? What might help it be successful? How might this relationship be detrimental? Is there anything you can do to prevent this?

Lesson 2
No One Is Like Him!

Daily Readings:
**Exodus 15:11; 1 Samuel 2:2; Isaiah 6, 46:9, 55:8-9;
Hosea 11:9; Revelation 4-5**

WARM UP

Just a couple of nights ago, I enjoyed watching the NCAA football championship. With the Heisman Trophy winner quarterbacking one of the teams, expectations were high, as the two top teams in the country battled for the crown. After a nail-biting end to the game, I listened to a panel of sports commentators provide their impressions of the hard-fought contest. One analyst remarked that the Heisman Trophy quarterback typically "transcends the game," but in this game, he only appeared "normal."

With all our biases, flaws, and weaknesses, transcendence is probably a poor term to use in describing another human being. Off-days occur in everyone's life, and the circumstances that surround them are often out of our control. Such is not the case with God.

Uniqueness of God

When God declares, "For I am God, and there is no other; I am God, and there is no one like Me" (Isaiah 46:9), He is proclaiming His holiness. The term "holy" in the Hebrew and Greek (*qadosh* and *hagios*) has the connotation of separation, uniqueness, and something that is set apart. So, in one regard, when we talk about God as holy, we are recognizing His uniqueness. Hannah's expression of praise to God in 1 Samuel 2:2 fittingly captured this concept. To her, "no one" was like the Lord. He is unique, truly one-of-a-kind.

Few in Scripture could lay claim to the type of relationship that Moses experienced with God. Raised in a culture that worshiped an array of gods, he serves as an excellent witness to God's uniqueness. Moses encountered God's extraordinary nature through a number of remarkable events and displays of power, such as the burning bush, the ten plagues, and the pillars of cloud and fire that went with Israel during the Exodus from Egypt. But his experiences with God culminated when the Lord parted the Red Sea, letting Israel walk across on dry land, and then collapsing the walls of water upon Pharaoh's army. Astonished by God's mighty deed, Moses and Israel sang a song of praise to their Savior and proclaimed, like Hannah, that no one is like the Lord (Exodus 15:11). No man, no angel, no god (if there were any), nor anything can compare to the Almighty. He is "majestic in holiness."

Scripture certainly attests to God's holiness, but what justifies attributing such a lofty trait to Him? Basically, the rationale is quite simple - God is the Potter, and we are malleable clay in His hands. God's separateness is a natural consequence of His position as Creator. As Master Designer of all things, He has no equal. He is in a category all by Himself, separate from the created realm. God is Creator; we are the created. Thus, God transcends or is above His creation.

God himself stated how He transcends one of humankind's remarkable abilities (Isaiah 55:8-9). God blessed us with a tremendous intellect. Our ability to innovate, design, reason, and understand difficult concepts is extraordinary. Nonetheless, God declared to Isaiah that His ways and thoughts far exceed our limited faculties to comprehend the scope of His purposes. Our know-it-all attitudes need to be checked at the door when we try to interpret the intentions of our Almighty Creator.

Holy Designations

Several writers in the Old Testament referred to God as "the Holy One" (e.g. Psalm 71:22; Proverbs 9:10). The title conveys His distinction over Israel as their Lord and Creator. God was above all; no other could merit such a title. In Hosea 11:9, God used this designation to distinguish Himself from humankind. Israel's security was grounded in the reality that *the* Holy One dwelt among them and yet experienced none of humanity's limitations. God's freedom and power was unconstrained by the impositions of the creation.

Isaiah's vision of the throne room of God shaped his concept of the Almighty (Isaiah 6). Not only did he see God majestically sitting on His throne, the Lord was attended by six-winged seraphim who thunderously praised Him. After being cleansed by one of the seraphim with a coal from God's altar, God commissioned Isaiah as a prophet. Undoubtedly, this vision profoundly affected Isaiah. While authoring the Book of Isaiah, he referred to God as "the Holy One of Israel" 25 times. To Isaiah, God certainly stood out as distinct.

Angelic Eyewitnesses

Angelic beings surrounded God in both Isaiah and John's throne room visions (Isaiah 6; Revelation 4-5). In each instance, these magnificent creatures offered up psalms of praise to honor their Lord. Standing in the Almighty's presence appears to naturally demand such a response. "Holy, holy, holy" were the first words that rolled off their lips (assuming they had them). In Hebrew, the repetition of holy three times designated that God's holiness was above all others. His holiness was absolute, and again, indicated that no one was like Him.

The seraphim in Isaiah's vision honored God's holiness in a couple of additional ways. In humility, they used two of their six wings to cover their faces, because they were in the presence of their Creator. They also took two of their wings and reverently covered their feet, since God's presence dictated that they stood on holy ground.

Later in John's worship-filled scene (Revelation 4:10-11), the 24 elders fell down before God's throne and cast their crowns by their sovereign's feet, lauding His creative powers in another psalm of praise. Displaying delegated crowns of authority has no place in the presence of *the One* who is the source of all authority - all honor is due Him.

COOL DOWN

One of the biggest challenges facing churches today is to provide worship services that truly honor our holy God. Our culture's love affair with self has brought about some unwanted side-effects in conjunction with our corporate worship, as well as our personal times of devotion. When self starts to take center-stage, the *emphasis* of worship changes from honoring God to seeking knowledge for *self*-edification, techniques for *self*-improvement, *self*-gratifying worship experiences, and perhaps even opportunities for *self*-promotion. Prayers become a laundry list of our wants and desires. Our singing turns into meaningless repetition, and the Lord's Supper becomes an unconscious act of worship.

Without the proper view of God, and who we are in relation to Him, the results described above will be inevitable. Perhaps we have conformed God into our own image. Seeking a relationship that meets our needs, He becomes our servant. We must genuinely ask ourselves, are we guilty of trivializing God? Have we lost the psalmists' deeply held convictions that produced their meaningful words of praise? Are such phrases as "the Lord reigns" and "Holy is He" rich or empty in meaning to you? Such accolades naturally flow when our perspective of God includes His holiness.

Because God sent Jesus to redeem us, we certainly recognize His loving ways, but how might we also develop a proper view of His holy nature. First, many stories in God's Word reveal that His power, greatness, and majesty are unsurpassed. Reading such stories as the Creation and Exodus through the lens of what they teach us about God's nature and our relationship to Him will bring about a new appreciation for our ominous God. Second, have you ever encountered God within His creation? God is a masterful designer and His artistic prowess is phenomenal. Reflecting upon who God is while experiencing His creation will bring you in touch with His holiness. Third, encountering God through the accomplishments of His people, and even what God has accomplished in you, can be enlightening. God empowers His people to accomplish His purposes, and God produces amazing results through ordinary people.

The stories of the angels give us hope. They are just created beings like you and me. Their worship is God-centered, participatory, and consists of heart-felt declarations that honor God's glorious nature. Properly understanding who they are in relation to the Almighty compels them to praise Him. We should aspire to their excellence in worship.

I once was told of a noble woman who started to prepare for worship on Saturday night. Evaluating our motives and preparing our hearts to properly engage in worship is a wonderful idea. Visualize the throne for worship's tone - you are in the presence of the Creator and Ruler of the universe. No one is like Him!

Questions

1. Genesis tells us that humanity is made in the image of God (Gen. 1:27). How then is God distinct and separate (holy) from humankind?

2. We could actually classify the seraphim of Isaiah's throne room vision as holy, but how do their behaviors point us to God's holiness? What should we learn from the angelic realm as to worshiping our holy God?

3. Have you ever felt that you encountered God through any of your life experiences? What specifically prompted such an insight? How did you respond?

4. Do you feel your congregation does a good job at honoring God's holiness during the worship service? How about you personally? What could be done to enhance this aspect of your worship? What can you do to better prepare yourself?

5. What aspect of our culture do you think influences our worship in a destructive way? Why is this the case? How should we address it?

6. Do your personal devotions ever include any aspects of worshiping God? What might you do differently? How do you think this might impact your spiritual formation?

Lesson 3
One Hundred Percent Pure

Daily Readings:
James 1:13-14; Habakkuk 1:13; Leviticus 19:2; Exodus 19:5-6; Matthew 5:20-48.

WARM UP

One of my pet peeves in life is to be served orange juice with ice. Distracted by the stresses of flying, this often happens when I ask for OJ on a plane. As the ice melts and dilutes the flavorful juice, its taste becomes unappealing to me. The bottom line is that I want "pure" OJ for both taste and health reasons.

In a similar manner, we humans tend to "dilute" who we truly are. Whether trying to conform to our peers' likes or disguise a character-istic that may not be popular, we don masks to cover our inner-self. And on occasion, we may go against our true nature which, over time, might even become corrupted. Thank goodness this is not the case with God. His holiness is not subject to corruption. He is totally true to His nature – 100% pure holiness.

In the previous lesson, we determined that God's holiness pertained to His uniqueness and transcendence; but Scripture also extends this concept of separateness to His moral (or ethical) purity. Evil and sin are in total opposition to His holy character.

Temptation-free Eyes

One of the most amazing traits of God is that He is not tempted to sin (James 1:13). For us temptation-prone humans, such a quality is hard to imagine. Whether knowing a juicy tidbit about someone, innocently viewing a TV show with risqué scenes, or not wanting others to think ill of us because of something we did, the lure of temptation starts to take form. Thoughts of gossiping, sexual improprieties, and lying may come to mind. However, because of God's perfect moral holiness, nothing holds this sway over Him. No bait can be dangled in front of Him that would tempt Him to do anything against His ethically pure nature.

Israel's God stood distinct from the gods of other religions in that He never followed the pathways of sin. Stories concerning the gods of paganism are filled with their sinful antics. All kinds of evil marred the character of these inept gods; deceit, murder, violence, adultery, and the like. Why would anyone want to put their faith in a god whose nature is so filled with ambiguities? With God, we can have great confidence in placing our faith in Him, since His pure holy nature allows Him to only deal righteously with us. It is exactly for this reason that Habakkuk trusts in the Lord, since His "eyes are too pure to approve evil" (Habakkuk 1:13).

Ethical and Moral Perfection

In the midst of Leviticus' holy requirements for the people of Israel, God provided the rationale for wanting them to adhere to a particular lifestyle. He emphatically stated that His nature is one of holiness, and to maintain fellowship with Him, they needed to embody this same quality (Leviticus 19:2). Holiness in this regard does not mean God's transcendence or His uniqueness amongst His creation. Obviously, such a request would be well beyond humanity's grasp.

God's call to holiness in this verse pertained to laws dealing with sexual conduct, social norms, business ethics, and the daily practices to follow to keep His people pure. By putting forward such laws, God indirectly informed us as to His ethically and morally pure nature. For God to dwell among the Israelites, they would truly need to become a holy nation (Exodus 19:5-6). God's absolute moral purity demanded His people also take on this quality. That of course is why God set up sacrificial requirements for the atonement of sin. Undoubtedly, just like us, the Israelite's shortcomings would lead to their stumbling.

In the Sermon on the Mount (Matthew 5-7), Jesus explained to His audience that a legalistic approach to righteousness would keep them out of the kingdom of heaven (5:20). He demonstrated within six examples (5:21-48) that just because someone correctly understands the Law, it does not necessarily mean that their heart is righteous. One can view the Law as a set of hard, cold rules and not embody any of the godly principles that stand behind them. So as in Jesus' examples, hurtful anger, sexual lust, spousal disloyalty, deceit, vengeance, and hate may still rule one's heart even though a specific law is obeyed on a particular occasion. Such a nature is totally contrary to God's and will inevitability corrupt our behavior.

I would like for you to note that all of Jesus' examples pertained to moral and ethical principles concerning relationships with others. It is important to keep this in mind as Jesus summarized His line of reasoning for His listeners; "Therefore you are to be perfect, as your heavenly Father is perfect" (5:48). As Jesus echoed the formula of Leviticus 19:2, He called believers to conformity with God's moral/ethical perfection, i.e. His holiness. Jesus set a moral goal for us to reflect His Father's holy character, and thus righteous behavior would naturally flow from a transformed heart. Jesus' intent is not to frustrate us with the unachievable goal of sinless perfection, but to encourage us to a life of godliness.

COOL DOWN

One of the dangers faced by living in a culture with worldly values is that our sensitivity to sin may become dull. In several of the psalms of David, he utterly disdains sin. Not that David was perfect, but the thought of evil and viewing sin appeared to hurt his holy conscience. Perhaps this is one of the reasons why God designated him as a man after His own heart.

Our eyes should always be sensitive to sin, injustice, and the plight of others in this world. Eyes empowered by a holy heart should be appalled at the sight of sin and the unjust treatment of others. One must ask - what dangers exist for the Christian whose eyes are not troubled over such things? With sin so prevalent, has the world's approach to life actually become a new standard to justify our future actions? Or perhaps a particular sinful lifestyle has started to become appealing. Conforming to society's unholy ways will be an ever-present issue for God's people. Another prevalent concern is the onset of indifference. Rather than feeling compassion for someone who has endured unfair treatment, has indifference relegated us to inaction? How our eyes perceive sin and injustices should be a good indicator as to whether we have a holy disposition, along with providing us a repulsive force to resist society's enticements.

Have you ever given much thought to the importance of believing in a holy God? What does it mean to your faith and hope that you believe in a God who is absolutely pure in all His ways? What if God had a few chinks in His armor, could you rely on Him? What if He swore to David that he would be successful in battle, only to let the Philistines overrun his army? Could we trust His promises? Could we trust Him to be fair with us?

When I was a manager at NASA, I had to make decisions that affected the safety of others and NASA's multi-billion dollar assets. It was crucial that individuals tell me the absolute truth pertaining to the problems we encountered with the flight systems, at least as they understood it. I learned the hard way though that some people have a tough time doing this. They feel they must tell you something to save face, even if it is wrong, rather than admitting that they did not know how a system worked or was behaving. Saying "I do not know, but I'll go find out" is a fair answer. But once someone ever knowingly fed me errant information, an important trust was broken. In the future, I would seek out others to validate their account. I would like to suggest that if God is not holy, you would seek other things in life in which to place your faith. Thank goodness we have a holy God in whom we can place the utmost confidence.

In the lessons to come, we will look at how holiness is developed, but for now, an examination of our behavior would be wise. Do you consider how you conduct yourself as ethical and moral? Think over some of your specific behaviors during the past week. What motivated your actions? Has any form of lust played a role in your thought processes? Pray that God will reveal any unholy ways that tend to control you.

Questions

1. What is meant by claiming that God is ethically and morally pure?
2. In choosing to follow God, does it make a difference to you that God is 100% ethically pure? What if He was not? Explain.
3. Have your eyes become dull to the world's participation in various sins? Has watching TV through the years dulled your senses to what is acceptable behavior? (see Jeremiah 8:12) What concerns should we have with this?
4. Many Christians may not exhibit negative behaviors but may have an attitude of indifference toward sin and the plight of others? Is this a problem? In what situations have you witnessed this? What might this indicate about our spiritual health?
5. Are there biblical principles that you wholeheartedly believe in yet have had a tough time living up to? What do you think might be the problem?
6. What advantages do we have in holy living that were not available to the Israelites under the Law?

Lesson 4
Jesus and the Holy Spirit

Daily Readings:
Luke 1:35, 4:31-35; John 6:66-69, 10:22-39; Acts 3:11-15, 4:23-31; 1 Corinthians 6:15-20; Ephesians 4:25-32; Hebrews 1:2-6; Revelation 3:7

WARM UP

Nicknames typically bring to light an interesting attribute, mannerism, or passion about the individual so "thoughtfully" dubbed. Of course not all nicknames are complimentary, but most of my friends and colleagues endear themselves to these descriptive titles. Years back, my officemates and I pegged one of our coworkers with the nickname "the Spirit." Every time some serious work came our way, he amazingly was nowhere to be found. Since he was not there to directly help us, we jokingly would say that he must be with us in spirit. I'm not sure if he ever knew the genesis of the name, but it was fairly descriptive of his behavior.

In a more serious tone, yet in a similar manner, God's Word provides us with a designation that uniquely suits and defines the nature of our Savior.

Jesus' Holy Designation

To help develop sound opinions on important matters, we pay particular attention to eyewitnesses and individuals with special knowledge. Obviously, no one wants to make judgments from hearsay. So to help build our faith, God provided us with various evidences to help ground our beliefs. Yet on occasion, some sources make us cock our heads in wonder.

Early in Jesus' ministry in a Capernaum synagogue, He was teaching on the Sabbath, when suddenly a man with a demon noisily interrupted Him (Luke 4:31-35). Concerned about Jesus' intention towards him, the unclean spirit revealed Jesus' divine identity as the "Holy One of God." Luke records this not as some casual observation, but with the force of direct knowledge.

But how does a demon acquire such information? Perhaps he possessed supernatural knowledge of Jesus' identity, but a more likely explanation is that he had personal familiarity with this Holy One of God. Since he came from the spiritual realm, this fallen, malevolent spirit surely had awareness of God the Son. This demon owed his created existence to Jesus, because nothing has come into being apart from Him (John 1:3; Colossians 1:16). Along with the angels, this demon may have witnessed Jesus' role in creation eons ago, such as when they shouted for joy as God fashioned the earth (Job. 38:4-7).

Luke presented an interesting bit of irony in his follow-up work of Acts concerning belief in the Holy One of God. After Peter healed a lame man by one of the temple's gates, a crowd gathered around him (Acts 3:11-15). Once shy of such opportunities, spirit-empowered Peter eagerly addressed the growing throng of amazed bystanders. He told them that the man was healed in Jesus' name, and this Jesus, whom they failed to recognize, was "the Righteous and Holy One." Identified by a demon, yet unrecognized by God's own people – kind of a sad state of affairs. Do we accurately recognize Jesus today?

Fortunately, a demon was not the only one to declare that Jesus was the Holy One of God. After witnessing numerous miracles by Jesus and experiencing the power of his teaching, Peter confessed that Jesus had the "words of eternal life" and was "the Holy One of God" (John 6:68-69). This knowledge had not come to Peter overnight but developed over time as an eyewitness to Jesus' ministry.

What is actually meant by referring to Jesus as the Holy One of God? Regrettably, Scripture does not provide us with a precise meaning, but some strong inferences are available to us. In Luke's account, the Holy One of God is likely related to Gabriel's announcement to Mary that she would bear the Christ-child. Because God was literally the Father, Jesus was considered a holy offspring and would be called "the Son of God" (Luke 1:35). Since "the" Holy One begat Jesus, the Son literally was the Holy One of God.

In John's Gospel, the Holy One of God also carries messianic overtones. At the Feast of the Dedication, the Jews pressured Jesus to reveal whether He was the Christ (John 10:22-39). Eventually in the conversation, He stated that along with being the Son of God, He had been set apart (sanctified) by His Father and "sent into the world" (vs. 36). Thus, Jesus had been sent as the Christ, a holy Savior, to redeem a lost world whom His Father loved.

Other Claims of Holiness

Teaching about Jesus landed Peter and John in jail on one occasion (Acts 4). After being brought before the Sanhedrin to determine their fate, these bold Apostles were released but warned to no longer speak of this "so-called" Jesus. Once Peter and John rejoined the rest of the disciples, they petitioned God in prayer to allow them to boldly preach the gospel despite the threats. During the prayer, they twice referred to Jesus as the "holy servant Jesus" (vs. 27,30). With Scripture's fulfillment and God's anointing, their prayer portrayed Jesus as the Christ. In this context, Jesus as the "holy servant" was the one whom God set apart to come to earth as the Christ and loyally suffer at the hands of the Jewish elite and the Romans.

When Jesus dictated to John the letter to the church in Philadelphia, He used the authorial name, "He who is holy" (Revelation 3:7). Such a claim is significant, as it puts His holiness on par with His Father's. With such an author, this would probably be a piece of mail that most of us would read.

In summary, Jesus' holiness was a reflection of His Father's holy nature, and indicated that He had been set apart by God to enter the world as the Christ. I think it is fair to say that Jesus is distinct and transcendent from the rest of creation just like His Father. Of course, Jesus' behavior was holy as well, but we will explore that in a future lesson.

The Holy Spirit

With the name "Holy" Spirit, one might ask, why are we discussing His holiness? The Holy Spirit is God's Spirit (2 Corinthians 3:3), so naturally He embodies God's holiness. In concert with Habakkuk's declaration concerning the purity of God's eyes (Habakkuk 1:13), Paul mentioned that the Spirit is actually grieved by our unholy attitudes and behaviors (Ephesians 4:25-32). Paul, in 1 Corinthians 6:15-20, also informed us that the Holy Spirit has taken up residence in each individual Christian, and our body is now His temple. And since sins of immorality are against the body, we bring this holy temple in direct contact with the unholy - Paul states, "May it never be!"

COOL DOWN

Typically as Christians, we gravitate toward warmly thinking of Jesus as a friend and brother. We want our relationship with Him to be personal and intimate. While this is appropriate and desirable, do we ever factor into this relationship that Jesus is holy? The writer of Hebrews lists several qualities of Jesus that separate Him from the rest of creation which serve to help us understand His divine holiness. Jesus is the heir of all things, agent of creation, glory and image of God, sustainer of all things, purifier of sins, and exalted to the right hand of God (Hebrews 1:2-3). Most certainly, the Holy One of God is a fitting title for our beloved Savior.

Is Jesus only your friend and brother? What of your confession of faith? Do you recognize Him also as your Lord? God has enthroned Jesus at His right hand. He now wears the titles of King of kings and Lord of lords (Revelation 19:16). God handed over the responsibility to Jesus to preside over the church – it's Christ's church, not ours. We need to recognize these attributes of Jesus, along with the warmer qualities we longingly seek.

As the author of Hebrews continues in the first chapter, we learn that we are not the only ones who may not always properly honor Jesus. The recipients of this letter had obviously placed the angels on a pedestal above Jesus. After demonstrating how Jesus was superior than the angels, the Hebrews' writer concluded that the heavenly hosts should worship Him (vs. 6). We need to also bow with the angels. "Worthy is the Lamb" should roll off our lips like the angels in the heavenly realm (Revelation 5:9-12). His holiness demands it.

Questions

1. Why do you think Luke records the words of the demon in Luke 4:34? How do you think the demon came by the knowledge that Jesus was the "Holy One of God?" Can we reconcile using this demon's witness today? Explain.

2. Reflecting on how you might typically describe Jesus, does holiness come to mind or is that an attribute we normally use to describe God? Why might this be the case?

3. List all the facets of Jesus' nature that make Him holy. Do you feel you adequately honor Jesus as the Holy One of God?

4. How might you change your worship to honor Jesus' holy nature?

5. Have you ever thought of how your attitudes and behaviors might actually be a source of grief to God's Spirit? Does it bother you to cause the Spirit grief? How might you use this knowledge to aid your spiritual formation?

Lesson 5
Holy Ones

Daily Readings:
Romans 1:7; 1 Corinthians 1:2; 1 Peter 2:9-10;
Ephesians 5:3-12; Psalm 89:5-7, 103:20-21; Daniel 4:13-17;
1 Thessalonians 3:13, Jude 6, 14; 2 Peter 2:4

WARM UP

Most of us desire to be aligned with something we consider special or worthy. Due to our involvement with these causes and activities, we may be labeled in a particular way. Though some may be negative, most labels we typically wear with pride, because they characterize what we view as important. Such designations can profoundly shape our identity, and how we want others to perceive us. Whether conservative, liberal, animal rights advocate, athlete, spiritual, caregiver, musician, or whatever your choosing, these designators possess defining-power and quickly convey to others some of our significant life orientations.

When I was younger, my desire to be associated with particular sports passionately gripped my soul. After making the basketball team in high school, we were allowed to wear our warm up jackets to school on game days. Hog heaven only begins to describe where I dwelt on those blessed days. To my way of thinking, wearing those school-colored jackets distinguished me as special and cried out "athlete" and "basketball player." In no uncertain terms, these characterizations significantly influenced my behaviors; sometimes in unhealthy ways.

Pursuing such worldly categorizations can create some negative traits in us, but God's Word contains a particular designation that, if personified, will only produce goodness.

WORK OUT

Literally speaking, Christians and angels are defined as "holy ones" in God's Word. The term typically translated by the NASB and KJV as "saints" is derived from the word for holy. The NASB usually translates this term as "saints" when applied to God's people and "holy ones" for angels. The KJV typically uses "saints" for both, though not always. So caution must be used when seeing these terms, recognizing the need to consider the context to determine the author's intent.

God's Holy People

Do you consider yourself of saintly status? The term "saint" is a great example of how the meaning of a word can change over time. No individual in the Bible is ever referred to as a saint. Titles like Saint Matthew or Saint Peter are non-existent in the biblical text. When referring to believers, this word is always plural, indicating that a community of believers is meant. It is a shame the original meaning has become obscured and is a point of confusion today.

In Romans 1:7, Paul addressed his Roman audience as "all who are beloved of God...called as saints." Paul was not singling out a group of religious elite that had meritoriously achieved some level of moral goodness. He was addressing all believers in the Roman Christian community. In fact, the designation "saints" was not based on some achievement by the believer – they were "called" by God (1 Thessalonians 2:12, 4:7).

Paul opened his first letter to the Corinthians by noting two hallmarks of its church members. They were considered "sanctified in Christ Jesus" and "saints by calling" (1 Corinthians 1:2). This terminology indicated the status that God had bestowed on them due to their acceptance of Christ. Set apart by God, the Corinthian believers were now His holy people dedicated to serve Him. Peter compared the Christian's lot with that of the Jews; they are chosen, priests, holy, and God's own (1 Peter 2:9-10). Peter then pointed out that these designations were not the result of human achievement but rather the product of God's mercy. Belonging to the holy people of God qualifies us all equally as saints.

Even though the God-given status as "saint" primarily designates a life of separation to God, it secondarily implies that one's walk should be consistent with this holy calling. In other words, by the very nature of who we are, God's holy people should exhibit holy character and behavior. Paul told the Ephesians not only to distance themselves from ungodly behavior, but that they needed to avoid even talking about such shameful activities (Ephesians 5:3-12). Unfortunately, our promiscuous and permissive society creates an unholy minefield that we must daily navigate.

Angelic Holy Ones

Since God's people share the designation of holy ones (saints) with the angels, that places us in pretty good company. Just as Christians have been set aside as holy servants to God, the angels join us in this noble calling (Psalm 103:20-21). Throughout Scripture, angels are seen serving God in various capacities; delivering His messages, executing His judgments, extending His compassion, protecting His people, and attending to Him at His throne. The term "holy one" shows up in conjunction with the angels carrying out their role as servants. In Nebuchadnezzar's vision, it was a "holy one" that delivered God's judgment against this self-glorifying king (Daniel 4:13-17). And when Jesus returns at the onset of the End Times, thousands of His "holy ones" will accompany Him to carry out the activities associated with the Judgment (1 Thessalonians 3:13; Jude 14).

Along with several of the biblical authors, Jesus himself referred to the angels as holy (Mark 8:38). And Cornelius's servants told Peter that Cornelius had been directed by a "holy" angel to summon him to his home (Acts 10:22). Those who represent God, need to be holy. In Revelation 14:10, we see that even angels refer to their compatriots as holy.

Due to their holy status, the angels stand in God's presence and have witnessed His majesty and mighty works through the ages (Psalm 89:5-7). To these privileged heavenly hosts, no one compares to God Almighty, so the "holy ones" of heaven praise and revere the Most Holy One. Even though standing in God's presence is a glorious honor for the angels, it comes with a weighty responsibility. Jude and Peter refer to an instance where angels made sinful choices which resulted in their banishment to pits of darkness until the Judgment (Jude 6 and 2 Peter 2:4) (See the author's book, *An Angel's View*, for a discussion of this subject).

Have you ever wondered how Paul could address the members of the Corinthian church as saints? Most churches today would most likely distance themselves from such a group. Plagued by issues associated with divisive factions, immorality, idolatry, Christians litigating against Christians, and one-upmanship, this church was a mess. "Saints;" come on Paul! How about heathens? I would guess not too many of you would be chomping at the bit to place membership at this church.

Nevertheless, Paul referred to these struggling Christians as saints; declared holy by God and separated to Him. Some definitely needed to repent of their misconduct, but Paul knew the power of God's grace. He may have his work cut out for him in leading the Corinthians to maturity, but he was obligated. These fledgling believers were God's own.

This should bring comfort to most of us, because, in reality, many of us are a mess. My weaknesses still raise their ugly heads now and then and cause me to stumble. I am just thankful God is patient with me, and Jesus' blood continues to cleanse me as I turn to Him. The group Mercy Me released a song a few years back called "Spoken For." A particular line in the chorus has deeply touched me through the years. The songwriter imagines God spotting him in the world and saying, "This one's mine," his "heart is spoken for." It brings tears to my eyes to think of God viewing me in such a way. We need to ponder such thoughts. Redeemed by an unfathomable love, we are God's own. Our hearts are spoken for.

Yet the angels' fall serves to remind us that our God is a holy God, and behavior corresponding to one's holy status is crucial to maintain a relationship to Him. He can not tolerate unholiness in His presence. God's holiness was in plain view to the angels, and thus they have no excuse or a redeemer (Hebrews 2:16). No hope remains for these angelic rebels. Humanity's lot is one of holiness as well, and God has revealed His holiness to us through His Son. Our redeemer's blood has separated us as God's people and through His life we have a reflection of God's holy ways. What a great hope we possess in Jesus.

"Spoken For" Words and music by Peter Kipley and Mercy Me. Copyright 2002, songs from the Indigo Room by Wordspring Music, Inc.

Questions

1. If you had to describe yourself with a few labels, what would you choose? Why did you choose these specific designations? Do you think others perceive you this way?

2. What do you typically think about when you hear the word saint? Now that you know this word is a descriptive title for all God's people, how do you feel about being called a saint/holy one?

3. Do you feel your life is consistent with the status of being a "holy one?" What do you need to do to personify such a title?

4. What do we learn about God from the angels' fall as described in Jude and 2 Peter? What does it teach us earthly holy ones?

5. Knowing at times church life can be messy, what should your approach be in helping a church through its struggles and living up to its holy calling?

Lesson 6

The Onset of Holiness

Daily Readings:
1 Corinthians 1:18-31, 6:9-11; Romans 6:3-18;
Hebrews 10:10-14, 29, 13:12; 1 John 1:5-10; Proverbs 21:2

WARM UP

After the Mars Pathfinder landed on our neighboring red planet, our Center Director at the Kennedy Space Center asked me to chair a group of out-of-the-box thinkers called the Exploration Think Tank. Chartered to identify key technologies that would eventually enable human missions to Mars and to initiate some start-up projects, this was one fun assignment. Sending humans to Mars was a matter of the heart for our Center Director, so he supported me in an unprecedented fashion for such a forward-looking activity.

Due to my new positional status, doors started to open, resources became available, and most important of all, I had ready access to my zealous Director who took great interest in what we were doing. In the past, scheduling an audience with him was next to impossible because of his busy schedule. After being appointed to my new position, I periodically met with him and could call on him pretty much as needed. Granting such access to me allowed him to facilitate our success through the various means available to him that were unavailable to my team.

As Christians, we have a zealous Leader, as well as One who takes great interest in our daily walk. Endowing us with new positional status, God stands ready to facilitate our eternal success.

WORK OUT

We mentioned in Lesson 5 that believers are "holy ones" or "saints," that is God has separated His people out as His own; they are holy and wholly His. In the various translations, several different words are associated with this activity by God, such as sanctification, sanctify, or holiness. Sanctification sounds daunting but just refers to God's work of making the believer holy. Because God's sanctifying work is sometimes referred to in a past tense and at other times appears to describe an ongoing progression, God's Word can leave us scratching our heads as to what is meant. So it is important to recognize that sanctification has two connotations in the New Testament. At times, it refers to the positional status of a believer's holiness, which we will discuss in this lesson. On other occasions, sanctification refers to the lifelong progression of bringing about holy character in the believer. This will be the topic of the lessons that follow.

Inception of Holiness

What enables the Christian to receive his new positional status as holy? Only the blood of Jesus can bring about this holy state

(Hebrews 13:12). There is nothing we can do to achieve this desired position. Jesus' bodily sacrifice made our sanctification possible. Only through His offering at the cross are God's people cleansed, purified, and perfected, i.e. made holy and enabled to have a relationship with our holy God (Hebrews 10:10-14).

In 1 Corinthians 1:18-31, Paul stated that the gospel message of a crucified Christ demonstrated the wisdom of God. Expecting the Messiah to be an earthly king to deliver them from the Romans, the Jews viewed a crucified Christ as nonsense. To the Gentiles, a god allowing himself to die as a criminal by the lowly means of crucifixion was also foolishness. But Christ crucified is the wisdom of God, because it solves the dilemma of our sinful spiritual state. Only through Jesus' sacrificial death can humanity obtain righteousness, holiness, and redemption, all of which are necessary to re-establish our relationship with God.

So when do we specifically come into contact with the blood of Jesus and receive our holy standing? This occurs at the beginning of our Christian life, our conversion. In Romans 6:3-7, Paul appears to indicate that this occurs at our baptism. After becoming united with Jesus in His death at baptism, we then are raised to a new life. Our "body of sin" is eradicated, and we never have to let it control us again. Upon being raised from the waters of baptism, we are not only soaking wet, but a new creation; a saint, a holy one of God. Baptism is our faith response for what Christ accomplished for us.

Foundation for a Life of Holiness

To urge the Corinthian Christians to pursue morally and ethically pure lifestyles, Paul reminded them of their sanctified standing in Christ (1 Corinthians 6:9-11). For Paul, moral obligation must be a consequence of one's holy status before God. Our holy standing should motivate us to pursue in practice, the holiness in which God has placed us, and of course, it also positions us to receive help from God in overcoming our corrupt ways. Removing sin and its stain was not God's end-game for His people, but transforming them to live a new holy life.

COOL DOWN

Most of us are not too fond of overhearing somebody demeaning an accomplishment of one our children. Even those crayon "master-pieces" hold great value to us, because they were the creation of one whom we dearly love. "Precious" is the only way to describe these works of art. Have you ever thought about how precious Jesus' ac-complishments were to God?

Hebrews 10:29 has always been a scary verse to me. To accept Christ in one's life, and then openly turn and rebel against Him leaves one in a terrifying quandary. However, within the severe language of this verse, we see God's love for His Son shining through. Jesus vol-untarily went to great extremes to redeem humanity. He selflessly endured tremendous suffering. His blood holds the very power that results in our holiness. For a Christian to regard it as unclean is inexcus-able betrayal. What Jesus achieved through the shedding of His blood is precious to God. A lot is at stake in what God accomplished through Jesus for us. We need to always hold His incomprehensible gift close to our hearts and treat it with the utmost esteem.

Not only does Christ's blood establish us in holiness, it has sustain-ing power as well. God's sanctifying provision does not stop at our conversion. He wants us to have confidence in our salvation throughout our lifelong journey. In 1 John 1:5-10, the Apostle John refers to God as light, which I believe to be a merging of the concepts of God's revealing quality of what is good and evil, and His extreme holy nature. To walk with God is to walk in the light. Or in other terms, true fellowship with God will reveal our imperfections as we strive to pursue holiness. Where we fall short and sin, Christ's blood continues to purify us and maintains our holy status before God. Sin will happen, confess it, keep pursuing God's holy ways, and He will be faithful and forgive us.

John plainly points out that sin is a characteristic of the Christian, but a lifestyle "controlled" by sinful passions (darkness) is not. In Romans 6:12-18, Paul explains to the Christians in Rome that they must be ever vigilant to keep sin from taking back control of their lives. Falling back into a state where they constantly obey their sinful lusts was unacceptable. When sinful passions overcome us and constantly control our actions, we are no longer walking in the light. Confession then becomes empty chatter to God. True repentance requires a turning from the sin that controls us and not allowing it to continue to reign. Without the pursuit of holiness (i.e. walking in the light) and genuine repentance, sin will become our new master and our positional holiness before God will be in jeopardy.

Wise old Solomon knew a person's ways were determined by the heart (Proverbs 21:2). Since we are fairly skilled at justifying and rationalizing away our actions, sometimes a corrupted heart may go unnoticed, even by ourselves. Solomon indicates that God takes an accurate measure of our hearts and understands the intentions behind our behavior. As we close this lesson, I'd like for you to ask God to reveal any sinful passions that may still have sway over you and to give you the moral courage to deal with them. Pray for God to put these passions to death and replace them with character traits that are pure.

Seek help from someone you view as spiritual who would be willing to lovingly hold you accountable for making progress.

Questions

1. In the course of life, have you ever had some type of positional status that served to help you in accomplishing your goals? How did it specifically aid you?
2. How do you view your holy standing with God? Does it affect how you view your daily walk? Explain.
3. What specifically sanctifies the Christian, i.e. gives us our holy status? How does this come about?
4. As Christians, if we turn back to a life of sin and openly rebel against Christ, will God deal with us differently than He does a nonbeliever? Explain.
5. Earnestly search your heart, do you feel that any unhealthy passions have taken control of your behavior or have the potential to do so? How could this affect your holy standing with God? What might your course of action be?

Lesson 7
A Lifelong Progression

Daily Readings:
Romans 6:17-23; 1 Thessalonians 4:1-7; 1 Peter 1:13-21; Hebrews 10:14

WARM UP

After graduating from the University of Central Florida with an engineering degree, NASA hired me to work in the Space Shuttle Program back in 1979. Once I showed up for my first day of work, I could legitimately claim that I was a NASA engineer (or rocket scientist as some like to call me). That was what my position description stated, so who could argue? But from a practical perspective, would making such a claim be accurate?

At this point in my career, I knew very little of what was required to safely accomplish human space flight. Designing systems to operate in the extreme environment of space was foreign to me. Exposure to how innovative redundancy schemes were utilized to survive failures was still in my future. "Green" only begins to describe my experience with our explosive and toxic propellants. Troubleshooting techniques for isolating problems in the Space Shuttle needed to be learned. And the sequence of events required to prepare and launch the Shuttle was still rocket science to this non-firing room tested new-hire.

Such knowledge and know-how resides at the core of what truly defines a NASA engineer. Yes, I was a NASA engineer when I initially hired on, but several years would pass before I truly "became" a NASA engineer. Quite a bit of mentoring, training, and time in the trenches would be required before I embodied the true nature of a rocket scientist.

WORK OUT

As mentioned in the previous lesson, sanctification not only refers to God setting us apart as holy at our conversion, but God's Word also speaks to sanctification as an ongoing activity. God grants to us a holy standing to have fellowship with us, but in practice, holiness becomes the Christian's lifelong pursuit (Hebrews 10:14).

The Upward Call of Holiness

In Romans 6:17-23, Paul contrasts a life controlled by sin with one led by righteousness. Enslavement to sin corrupts our character which ultimately results in spiritual death. On the other hand, if we lead a life controlled by righteousness (vs. 19) or God (vs.22), it yields holiness within us with an end-result of eternal life. Obviously, Paul is not referring to an individual's initial sanctification, but a lifelong pursuit. As the Christian progresses in developing a holy character, obeying God's will becomes a matter of a transformed heart.

Paul acknowledged that the Thessalonians had made good progress in their Christian walk, but urged them to still kick it up a notch (1 Thessalonians 4:1-7). To help motivate their desire to grow, Paul pointed out that developing a holy nature was God's will for them. Steeped in a sexually permissive pagan society, Paul wanted them to strive to escape their past immoral ways. Rings a little true of what we face in today's culture. Their immorality stood in stark contrast to God's aspiration for them. God had not called them to impurity, but "to live a holy life" (vs. 7, NIV). Again, in these verses, you can detect an ongoing activity, not only some past action by God.

By now you might be saying, "OK, I am to become holy, but please put some practical meat on these bones." Let's start going down that path.

A Way of Life

In 1 Peter 1:13-16, Peter called several Gentile churches to action in order to keep their hope of salvation alive through holy living. He asks them to "gird up your minds." With this phrase, Peter appears to have in mind the metaphor of gathering one's long robe and securing it to prepare for hard work. Today we would express such a notion as "rolling up one's shirt sleeves." But this girding is not for physical work; it is for the mind. Past desires and passions can easily resurface to overcome the mind. Exhibiting self-control ("keep sober") is crucial in keeping focused on the hope of salvation.

Peter informed his readers that they were to be like children, modeling their behavior after their Father. Of course their Father is none other than God, *the* Father. To emphasize the importance of following in His footsteps, Peter phrased his direction in both negative and positive terms. First, he warned them that continuing to conform to their culture's lustful habits was not an option, as it opposed their holy Father's nature. Since Peter makes multiple appeals in his letter to this regard, these Christians must have been experiencing a tough time breaking away from their society's excesses (ref. 2:11 and 4:2-4). He therefore instructs them to no longer be conformists, letting the lusts of a former life destructively control them.

Second, Peter expressed the need to exhibit holy behavior like the "Holy One" who called them. Since they were called by God, they were now His own. So He was to serve as their model, standard, and reason for holy living. The Greek term translated as "behavior" *(anastrophē)* literally means "way of life." Holy conduct is not just reserved for our times with the faithful, but should be demonstrated in *all* aspects of life. Holiness's impact does not just pertain to sexual purity, but permeates *all* behavior. For example, kindness replaces rudeness and honesty replaces deceit. A new orientation takes hold of us, bringing an ethical dimension to all that we say and do.

To ground his direction in absolute authority, Peter employed the voice of God (vs.16). The Almighty Himself told Israel in the Leviticus Code that His people should lead holy lives because He is holy (Leviticus 19:2). His principle remains unchanged; God's people in all times must strive to walk consistently in holiness. Remember from our earlier lesson that God's declaration to Israel in Leviticus occurred in the middle of His demands that they adhere to various ethical/moral standards. Even though, the Levitical Code's holy requirements serve as an example for his churches, Peter was not binding it on them. These Gentiles found their holiness rooted in, and lived out through, the redeeming work of Jesus (1 Peter 1:17-21), and the sanctifying work of the Holy Spirit (1:2).

COOL DOWN

Adopting holiness as a way of life has its distinguishing marks. Peter's concern primarily dealt with the ethical dimension holiness, but the quality of separateness still existed. Christians must separate themselves from their old futile way of life in order to follow God (1:15,18). Transformation to a new spiritual life is mandatory in order to produce godly behaviors in our daily walk. So in a culture that adheres to corrupted values, one who exhibits holy behavior becomes an "alien," distinct from the rest of society (1:1; 2:11).

Peter expected holiness to guide the Christian's behavior, which in turn also served to separate them from those who bow to the lusts of life. But Peter was not encouraging his hearers to physically isolate themselves from non-believers. Nevertheless, that is the very thing we tend to do. We construct islands, surrounded by shark infested waters to keep the world out.

Sometimes we may need a little alone-time to aid our spiritual growth, but Peter's strategy involved staying right in the mix of things. Christianity was to be lived out in a corrupted world. To Peter, not only does a holy way of life lead to personal salvation, but several other important results occur as the Christian conducts a godly life among non-believers – God is glorified (2:12), conversions are facilitated (3:1-2), and the Christian faith is made evident (3:16).

Of course the downside is that Christians will need to stand strong against temptations they will face. Developing a holy nature is critical, because it serves to quench the flames of lust. Remember, lust pertains to all forms of temptations, not just sexual desires. After overhearing a bit of personal information about a friend, a lust to gossip

46

may arise because of your desire to be accepted by others. Our holy nature would respect our friend and not entertain spreading potentially hurtful information about them.

Making progress in our pursuit of holiness may at times be a little frustrating. Our old passions have a way of haunting us. How to address them will be a topic in a future lesson. For now, I would like to ask, do you believe your behavior distinguishes you from others in the world? Based on your behavior alone, can those in the world detect that there is something different about you? Is there an inner motivation that calls you to live above the ethical standard of those around you?

Questions

1. Do you recall any title that you would have been uncomfortable claiming until you had achieved a certain level of proficiency? In your opinion, what traits do you identify with this title?
2. What drives an individual's behavior? What do you believe drives your behavior and how would you classify it?
3. Why is becoming holy important? Are you motivated by this as a God-given goal? Explain.
4. When Peter says we are to be holy like God, what is he specifically talking about? Should we expect this to occur quickly? Explain.
5. Peter expects our life of holiness to be lived out in the world. What negative outcomes might result if we try to isolate ourselves from the world? What positive outcomes should we expect if we do as Peter suggests?
6. Can you identify a couple things that create unhealthy desires in you? How are they contrary to the development of holiness? What should you do about it?

Lesson 8
The Goal of Holiness

Daily Readings:
1 Peter 1:14-16; 2 Corinthians 3:18, 4:4-6; Galatians 4:19;
Ephesians 4:13: Colossians 1:15, 3:1-17;
Matthew 6:19-24, 23:23; John 4:34

WARM UP

Establishing a life goal after breaking your neck may seem a little ominous. Aspirations concerning children, homes, or jobs might be more amenable for us to think about. My wife is a Physical Therapist who was rehabilitated from a broken neck that occurred in a gymnastic accident. Learning to walk again became a future target for her. Today, as she helps people recover from various accidents and surgeries, she aids them in developing goals for their rehabilitation. I remember her telling me of a woman who had sustained a serious shoulder injury whose goal involved reaching into the kitchen cabinet to obtain a drinking glass. Goals are relative. Our life circumstances often dictate our future aims.

Developing goals help us envision our possible future. Realism plays an important part in determining goals, but they need to stretch us past our current capabilities. Goals bring about focus to our daily activities and purpose to our lives. For the Christian, we need to recognize that God has set some goals for His people that are important to their spiritual well-being.

WORK OUT

By now you probably have figured out that 1 Peter 1:14-16 is thematic to this overall study. Peter points out that holiness is a goal of the Christian and should be evident in *all* our behavior. But our goal of holiness is extraordinarily lofty; it is to be like God's holiness! How do we ever understand all the facets of His holiness? Becoming like God in any regard is intimidating enough, and even more so when it is complicated by such an abstract concept.

Images

Paul tells us in 2 Corinthians 4:4-6 that the gospel literally sheds some light on this subject. The illuminating power of the gospel reveals that Jesus is a direct "image of God," and that God's glory is disclosed in Christ's image. Paul made these observations in support of his summary thought in 2 Corinthians 3:18. His point is that even though God's people cannot directly see Jesus today, His reflection is seen in the gospel story. When we behold Jesus, we see God's glory. So God's nature and behavior are revealed to us in His Son.

In 2 Corinthians 3:18, Paul made another crucial observation for our study. As we behold Christ's image in the gospel; it becomes the goal of the Christian's transformation. This transformation does not happen overnight, but is a lifelong progression (also see Romans 8:29, 12:1-2).

In the English language, we derive our word *metamorphosis* from this Greek word translated as "transformation." Our change is not inconsequential, but a radical one, like from a caterpillar into a butterfly.

Paul conveyed a similar thought in His letter to the Galatians, when he stated that the formation of Christ within them was driving him to expend energy like a mother in labor (Galatians 4:19). The Greek term Paul chose concerning formation typically involves the development of an embryo into an infant. Again, the spiritual development of God's people involves serious change. Maturing into the "fullness of Christ" is our end-goal (Ephesians 4:13). Expect a struggle at times, because we will have to defeat the "fullness of self" along the way.

Holiness and Image

I would like to suggest that the goal of holiness (or sanctification) is virtually synonymous with our transformation into the image of Christ. Not until we embody the characteristics of Christ do we stand a chance of being holy like God. In our pursuit of Christlikeness, God is working from the inside out. As we internally become more and more like Jesus, holy behaviors will begin to naturally flow, as our past worldly influences diminish their hold on us.

In Colossians 3:1-17, Paul basically appealed to the Colossians to turn from every form of unrighteous behavior to a new set of virtues that was consistent with their holy God. They were no longer worldly, because Christ resided in each of them (vs. 11) and had become their life (vs. 4). Since He was the image of God (1:15), Jesus became the pattern for their on-going restoration to the image of their Creator, or as Paul stated in 2 Corinthians 3:18, to the glory of God in the image of Christ.

The progressive renewal of the "new self" produces a "true knowledge" of God (vs. 10). This knowledge is not a compilation of facts about Him, but an understanding of who He is and what He is all about. Through Christ we can attain an understanding of God's will for us and the true intentions of His commands. As a result, the inner affections of our hearts are to be aligned with God's character, which includes compassion, kindness, humility, gentleness, patience, forgiveness, love, peace, and thankfulness (vs. 12-15). Out of such a heart, holy conduct will come forth; conduct consistent with our holy calling.

COOL DOWN

At this point, we could derive an extensive list of Christ's character traits from the gospels. Passages dealing with the fruit of the Spirit (Galatians 5:22-23) and the various Christian virtues might also prove helpful (2 Peter 1:5-7), but I am afraid we will barely scratch the surface if we tried to constructively study such a list. Instead, let's dive a little deeper into one of Jesus' lesser-discussed attributes – loyalty or faithfulness.

Disgust only begins to describe Jesus' attitude toward the hypocritical lifestyle of the scribes and Pharisees. To point out their convoluted way of life, Jesus provided seven examples that are often referred to as the "Seven Woes" (Matthew 23:13-36). In one of the illustrations, Jesus mentioned how these two-faced legalists nitpicked one another over the lesser matters of the Law while ignoring the more important ones (vs. 23). Do you think we ever squabble over the unimportant at the expense of the important? To leave no room for argument, Jesus highlights three prominent aspects of the Law – faithfulness, justice, and mercy. Obviously, faithfulness is an important attitude of the heart for us to develop.

We live in a society where fractured loyalties are commonplace. Consider the following; political party partisanship versus our country's best interest, union stances versus a company's profitability, a professional athlete's pursuit of money versus allegiance to their team and fans, and family time versus personal recreational priorities. Both sides of the above examples have their place, but you must admit that one's loyalties are often placed in tension and competed for today.

Jesus leaves no wiggle room for the Christian; divided loyalties are not an option (Matthew 6:24). Inevitably, they become incompatible. Our affections grow in the direction of one of our pursuits while the other becomes despised. The context of Jesus' comment concerned the divided loyalties that occur when simultaneously trying to pursue wealth/possessions and spiritual blessings (Matthew 6:19-24). One or the other will take control of the heart and drive our future actions. Have you ever experienced this dilemma?

Earlier in my life, playing competitive sports held an undue influence over me. Rather than looking out for the best interest of others, I found myself manipulating situations and people to satisfy my self-serving goals through the sport. Divided allegiances were taking a toll on my spirituality during this phase of my life.

Many biblical examples of loyalty have been recorded for our benefit, such as Shadrach, Meshach, and Abednego's skirt with death in the fiery furnace and Joseph's faithfulness under various trials. But no role model can equal that of our Savior. John's Gospel could actually be viewed as a treatise on Jesus' loyalty to His Father. Time after time Jesus attested to the fact that His works and teachings resulted from following God's will. He even described serving His Father as a culinary delight (John 4:34), i.e. it was spiritually nutritious. If faithfulness in following God's will was spiritually developmental for Jesus, do you not believe it will serve you in a similar way?

The holy character trait of loyalty to God produces faithful behavior in His people. Jesus took this attribute to the extreme in following His Father's will all the way to the cross. No other concern could derail Him. God expects the same from us. Like His Son, we are to be faithful until the end, and as a result, the Faithful One Himself will reward us with the crown of life (Revelation 2:10).

Questions

1. Can you recall any life goals that helped shape your character or behavior? Have you found any goals set forward in Scripture spiritually challenging? Explain.
2. Identify some areas where your character has changed since you became a Christian. To what extent have these areas changed? What still needs work?
3. Based on this lesson, what is God's plan for restoring us to His image?
4. What is meant by pursuing the American dream? Explain how it might work against faithfully following God's will?
5. Can you identify any life pursuit that has a strong influence on your heart? How might this be affecting you spirituality? Is there anything that could occur that would allow you to stay involved with this activity, while not allowing it to impact your faithfulness to God?
6. In your spiritual journey to date, can you identify any areas of your character that may have undergone radical transformation? Share with the class.
7. How might the pursuit of the American Dream affect our faithfulness in following Christ?

Lesson 9
Holiness and the Spirit's Role (Part 1)

Daily Readings:
Ezekiel 36:25-27; Jeremiah 31:31-34; Hebrews 10:10-18; 2 Corinthians 3:3-8; John 3:1-10; Matthew 15:18-19

WARM UP

Thinking about safety is not one of the more prevalent things on a recent college graduate's mind. But to work for NASA on the Space Shuttles, a concern for the safety of the astronauts, your co-workers, the public, and the flight hardware was a top priority. Being accountable for the lives of others and multi-billion dollar national assets was a weighty burden I suddenly found on my shoulders upon coming on-board with NASA. Learning the principles of safety did not take too long, but for it to become truly second nature would require a little more time.

NASA had a wonderful safety culture, going well beyond its motto of "Safety First." My mentor trained me in how safety was designed into the flight systems, and how to infuse it in every step of our test procedures. Training occurred throughout my career in toxic propellants and commodities, hazardous facilities and equipment, and safety principles and protocols. Safety became something I lived and breathed. But sometimes tragedy has a way of deepening our commitments.

Living through the Space Shuttle Challenger disaster resulted in my re-creation as a NASA engineer. Viewing the explosion over and over, hearing the ever-echoing final communication of astronaut Dick Scobee, recognizing the astronauts I had worked with were no longer with us, and realizing the horror the astronauts' families experienced had a tearfully sobering affect on me. Safety was no longer just a set of rules to be observed; it was now a matter of the heart.

WORK OUT

Even though the Law was holy and taught of holiness (Romans 7:12), it stood powerless to create holiness *within* the individual. God determined "Mission Holiness" (NASA-speak) would be required, but its cost was tragic. Requiring His Son's life, our loving God brought about the means to develop holiness in His people. It never ceases to amaze me what God has done to have a relationship with me.

Let's begin exploring how God facilitates our holiness by first looking into the Holy Spirit's role in developing this quality in a two-lesson study. Knowing His Apostles were saddened over His upcoming departure, Jesus told them that His leaving would be "advantageous" for them, because He would send the Holy Spirit (John 16:7). Think about that for a minute; what an extreme statement. The Spirit's benefit actually outweighs Jesus' physical presence. What the Spirit has to offer must be pretty incredible. Let's see what this promise holds for us today.

To the Heart of the Matter

During Israel's exile in Babylon, Ezekiel prophesied of a time, when God's people would be renewed and given the ability to follow His commandments (Ezekiel 36:25-27). To accomplish this, God needed to address the condition of the human heart. Time and again, the Jews failed to embody the essence of the Law and become holy like their God, so a new approach was necessary. God promised to give His people softer, pliable hearts, conducive to truly following and becoming like Him. But most importantly, success would depend on God placing His Spirit within His followers.

Jeremiah foretold of a time when God would create a new covenant with His people. God's laws were not only destined to reside on tablets of stone and scrolls, but God declared He would put them within His followers by writing them upon their hearts (Jeremiah 31:31-34). The author of Hebrews stated that this new covenant came about at Jesus' sacrifice on the cross (Hebrews 10:10-18).

Reminiscent of both the above prophecies, Paul basically told the Corinthian church that their new-found spirituality was evidence of the fulfillment of these prophecies (2 Corinthians 3:3-8). God's laws were no longer written on stone but on the Corinthians' hearts, and only the penmanship of "the Spirit of the living God" (vs. 3) could accomplish such a feat.

Ministry of the Spirit

Paul goes on to explain to the Corinthians that his ministry involved delivering the blessings of the new covenant. Since the old covenant held no power to internally change the individual, breaking the Law would be inevitable and would result in spiritual death. But Paul's ministry had the power to bring about change within its recipient. Spirit-powered, the new covenant brought spiritual life. Along with the Corinthians, Christians today reside in the era of the glorious "ministry of the Spirit" (2 Corinthians 3:8).

In John 3:1-10, Jesus explained to Nicodemus that to enter the kingdom of God one needed to be spiritually born again. Jesus referred to this twice as being "born of the Spirit" (vs. 6 and 8). Such a birth yields spiritual goodness. Jesus compared it to the wind, even though you may not understand where it comes from, you can observe its effect. So it is with the Spirit's activity within the human. You may not know how the Spirit has worked on the heart of another, but you can see the results from the fruit of their behavior.

Unfortunately for Nicodemus, Jesus' teaching was not "clicking" for him, and he asked, "How can these things be?" (vs. 9). As a teacher of God's people, Jesus found Nicodemus's lack of understanding reprehensible. But what did Jesus think Nicodemus should have known? To Jesus, a competent teacher of Israel should be familiar with the predictions of the prophets, and Nicodemus failed to recognize in Jesus' teaching that the fulfillment of Ezekiel's prophecy of spiritual renewal was at hand.

I guess we could say Jesus really nailed it when he promised that the Spirit would be beneficial. Citizenship in God's kingdom, spiritual life, and the ability to follow God's holy ways are all possible because of the gift of the Holy Spirit within us.

Write on Holy Spirit, write on!

COOL DOWN

In an upcoming lesson, we will look at *our* role versus the *Spirit's* in pursuing holiness. For now, a couple observations are important. First,

God is not going to "write" things on our hearts that we don't want there. Second, even though we are a new creation and given a new heart at conversion, the renewal process continues throughout our life. Becoming holy or like Jesus is not an overnight event.

Many of you at some point in your life had to endure a dress code. Most workplaces, schools, and even athletic teams have regulations concerning what you wear. Some of these rules have practical considerations while others are concerned with image or some societal norm. Most dress codes that involve our safety are not something we quibble about, but the ones concerning image and norms often create a little bit of anguish. Wearing closed-toed shoes made a lot of sense on our work platforms at the Kennedy Space Center, but does wearing a tie equate with professionalism?

Whatever the case, most of us willingly complied with these norm-oriented dress codes out of obligation, i.e. they were not a matter of the heart. We basically followed them because we were expected to and breaking such rules came with consequences. Losing a job over breaking a dress code seems pretty silly, and since most of us like our paychecks, we comply.

In a similar fashion, this is what happened with the Jewish nation and the Law. It became only a matter of obligation to obey it and not a matter of the heart. In the New Testament times, God has given us His Spirit to create willing hearts and to create a nature within us conducive to obeying His commands.

If we strive to make our Christianity a set of do's and don'ts, we can easily pour through God's Word in a manner that is not conducive to the development of the heart. Basically, it becomes only a matter of the mind and not the heart. You may exhibit the proper behaviors at times, but when things don't go your way or stressful situations arise, do you think holy behaviors will come forth?

Developing biblical knowledge is important, but if it is done while ignoring the heart, a corrupt spirituality will result. Remember, Jesus praised the Pharisees for knowing the Law, but condemned their hypocritical hearts and practices (Matthew 23:3ff). As Jesus said, the things that come out of the heart are what defile us (Matthew 15:18-19). Like the Jews, we have God's Word, but we also have His heart-shaping Spirit. Let's not neglect so great a gift.

Questions

1. How might it be more advantageous for Christians to have the indwelling Spirit than having Jesus on earth in the body?
2. What shortcoming of the Law caused God to use another approach to spiritually renew His people? Describe His new approach.
3. Based on this lesson, what benefits result from to the Spirit residing in the Christian?
4. We may not be able to totally understand how the Spirit works, but how do we know that He has been at work?
5. How might treating the Bible as a rule book impact your spiritual development?
6. How would you characterize a church or an individual that pursued knowledge at the expense of developing the heart? (See 1 Corinthians 8:1)

Lesson 10
Holiness and the Spirit's Role (Part 2)

Daily Readings:
1 Peter 1:2; 1 Thessalonians 4:7-8; 2 Thessalonians 2:13; Ephesians 3:16-19, 4:30; Romans 8:13; Philippians 2:12-13; Galatians 5:16-23; 1 Corinthians 6:19-20

WARM UP

Working on the Space Shuttle's Main Engines (SSME) at NASA was a dream job. The combined power generated by these three beasts maxes out at about 37,000,000 horsepower. How about that NASCAR fans? They create a combined thrust of a little over 1.2 million pounds during launch. If water was pumped by the turbo-machinery from just one of these engines, a typical backyard swimming pool could be emptied in about 25 seconds. What power! These Pratt-Whitney Rocketdyne- built engines are a tribute to American know-how and ingenuity.

Even though the mighty SSMEs are powerful enough to help propel the Space Shuttle into the heavens, they are powerless in helping humanity reach heaven. Through the Almighty's wisdom and ingenuity, He has equipped His people with a tremendous spiritual engine

– His own Spirit. We are a Spirit-empowered people, with the most powerful force in the universe ready to assist us in achieving our heavenly goal.

WORK OUT

From the time of our conversion, the Holy Spirit started His sanctifying work (1 Peter 1:2). He made us holy and set us apart as God's own people. However, His work was not complete. Paul tells us that the means to securing our salvation involves the on-going sanctifying work of God's Spirit in our lives, as well as our faith in the truth (we'll discuss our role in the next lesson) (2 Thessalonians 2:13). So let's look at what the Spirit is trying to accomplish in us.

Power to His People

We learned earlier from 2 Corinthians 3:18 and 4:4-6 that God is revealed to us through Christ in the gospel. As we behold Jesus in the gospel story, our hearts are enlightened and gradually transformed into His likeness. The passive voice in the Greek indicates that the transformation is not accomplished by us, but as Paul points out, it is the Spirit that brings about this change. Hearts written on by the Holy Spirit (3:3) facilitate the formation of Christ within us and enable holy behavior.

Paul expressed this a little differently in his prayer for those in the church of Ephesus (Ephesians 3:16-19). He requested that God empower their inner-being with the Holy Spirit. The initial goal of the Spirit's strengthening was for Christ to dwell in the Ephesians' hearts (vs. 17). Practically speaking, experiencing the Spirit's power was for Christlike character to be formed in their hearts to guide their daily lives.

Paul wanted the fertile ground of love to be the medium for the Ephesians' growth. Love-rich soil helps develop an understanding of the depth and dimensions of love's yearnings to sacrificially meet the needs of others at one's own expense. Such love was Christ's love, and Paul wanted them to personally know, i.e. experience this love (vs. 19). This was not some theological rambling by Paul. Experiencing Christ's love in his life changed him from a self-seeking religious zealot to an others-seeking servant of His Savior (2 Corinthians 5:14-15). He earnestly desired the same for the Ephesians.

Ultimately, the combination of the empowering of the Spirit, the indwelling of Christ in the heart, the fertile ground of love, and the personal knowledge of the love of Christ was to enable the Ephesians to "be filled up to the fullness of God" (vs. 19). Similar to the thought of 2 Corinthians 3:18, where Christ reflects the glory of His Father and through the work of the Holy Spirit, the very attributes of God become our own. Or in terms of our theme, the Christian becomes holy like their holy God.

God did not abandon us to our limited faculties in achieving holiness. He gave us the powerful gift of His Spirit to bring it about. Attaining holiness is a divine act of God through the agency of His Holy Spirit, as He works alongside, or should I say inside, His people.

Death and the Harvest

Approaching sanctification from a negative angle, Paul told the Christians in Rome that putting to death their sinful behaviors "by the Spirit" would bring them life (Romans 8:13). Note that this is a human initiated activity but accomplished through the power of God's Spirit. But what is the Spirit's actual role? A passage in Philippians sheds a little light on this. Paul instructed the Philippians to take on the daunting task of working out their salvation (virtually equivalent to becoming holy like God) while consoling them that they were not alone in tackling this challenge (Philippians 2:12-13). God Himself would be at work in them, strengthening their desire ("to will") and ability ("to work or act") to achieve this ominous objective. This passage is not insinuating that God makes us do something contrary to our will. Such a conclusion would go against Paul's theology elsewhere.

As we have seen, the Spirit help's bring about Christlike qualities within the believer, so a natural consequence of this activity would include a change in our desire (or "will") to participate in activities that go against our heart's new disposition. So the Spirit helps put to death our pursuit of a sinful lifestyle in two ways. First, because the Spirit is at work within us developing a Christlike character, a desire to pursue holiness begins to replace our past desires to pursue a sinful lifestyle. Second, the Spirit energizes our abilities to take on the task of putting to death our old sinful pursuits. For instance, we may be strengthened to replace an old temptation-filled activity with a new one that allows us to exercise our Christlike qualities. As you well know, putting aside sinful habits can be extraordinarily difficult. Look at the history of the Jewish nation in the Old Testament. Without the Holy Spirit actively working in our lives, a life of frustration is inevitable.

In Galatians 5:16-23, Paul revealed to the Galatian churches the consequences of pursuing a lifestyle led by the Holy Spirit versus the flesh. For the person who walks by the Spirit, a holy harvest results. Fruit of divine origin is its yield – "the fruit of the Spirit" (v.s 22). Such a crop is not the result of human endeavor by following the Law, and chasing fleshly desires leads to spiritual ruin. Walking by the Spirit is a faith-oriented activity and brings true life by producing fertile soil for the Spirit to grow these Christlike characteristics in the believer. When the qualities of love, joy, peace, and the like are embodied, holy behaviors will naturally flow, enabling us to be like our holy God.

Most of you probably remember the pain of moving into a new home. One of the first things you probably did was give the place a good old scrubbing. Not many enjoy this type of hard work, but your family's health and welfare motivated you to prepare a clean and germ-free environment for them to live in and thrive. Imagine how appalled you would be, if you later discovered that a child of yours had been throwing garbage on the floor of his room, virtually living in filth. As you entered their room, a sickening odor filled the air, maggots seethed from rotting food, and germs were the only thing thriving in these disgusting conditions. Desecration might be the first word to enter your mind.

In practicality, when you committed to God, He committed to you. As part of His commitment, He prepared a place inside you to dwell. We are not talking about some ordinary dwelling place, but a temple, a holy place befitting God's Holy Spirit (1 Corinthians 6:19). As part of your commitment, God expects you to not defile His temple. Your body is no longer yours, God paid for it with His Son's blood (vs. 20). Not that you won't stumble now and then, but God expects you to no longer practice sin.

Paul explains in 1 Thessalonians 4:7-8, that if we reject God's call for us to lead a holy life by continuing to practice sin, we in essence reject Him. This rejection is compounded because God placed His Spirit inside the Christian to accomplish what we have chosen to reject, our sanctification. The construction of the Greek in verse 8 emphasizes that the Spirit given is God's Spirit and is holy. Characterized by holiness with the job of creating holy attitudes within us, it is grievous to

God's Spirit to oppose His work and holy being by walking in our old patterns of sinful pursuits (Ephesians 4:30).

Perhaps, spiritually speaking, there really is something to the old adage, "Cleanliness is next to godliness." So honor God and keep His temple clean.

Questions

1. Have you ever been empowered by someone to accomplish a task? What specifically did the empowerment involve?
2. Reflecting on your life, how has your character changed? What brought about these changes?
3. Integrating some past passages we have studied, why can we say that working out one's salvation (Philippians 2:12) is virtually equivalent to becoming holy like God?
4. What is meant by experiencing Christ's love? Have you experienced it? How?
5. If God's Holy Spirit has taken up residence in you, what housecleaning do you need to do in order to honor and allow Him to do His work?
6. At this point, how would you explain the Spirit's role in creating holiness within the Christian?

Lesson 11
Holiness and Our Role

Daily Readings:
1 Peter 1:2; 2 Corinthians 7:1; Psalm 139:23-24;
Galatians 2:20; 2 Timothy 2:20-26; Romans 10:17;
Ephesians 2:10, 4:12; Matthew 20:28

WARM UP

Over the years, many people have commented to me about the wonderful technologies developed by NASA, and how a particular spin-off product has impacted their life. Taking a concept for an innovative technology through the stages of development to where a new product becomes available is no trivial matter. Many researchers come up with phenomenal ideas and are excellent at validating their concepts in a laboratory, but when it comes to engineering it into a useful product, they typically cry for help. Finding the right partner, who knows how to turn a researcher's idea into a technology that reliably works in a particular environment, is of paramount importance if one wants to thrive in the world of technology development. Partners seek ways to succeed together and look out for each other's best interests.

From the previous couple of lessons, we learned that our sanctification comes by way of the Holy Spirit. If such is the case (and it is), then how are we to interpret the verses that appear to place the "pursuing" and "perfecting" of holiness on our backs (Hebrews 12:4; 2 Corinthians 7:1)? Are we not then responsible? Most certainly, we will be held accountable, but rest assured that the Holy Spirit will also perform His part. Remember, holiness is God's goal for us, not an imposition. In essence, God has placed us in a partnership with the Spirit to achieve holiness in our lives. Our desires, actions, and conduct produce the soil for the Holy Spirit's nurturing activity. Fertile or unfertile, it's our choice. Let's look at a few fruitful ways to contribute to this partnership.

Prayer and Image

To develop a holy nature we must conform to Christ's image, but to accomplish this we must first understand our brokenness. Some of our character deficiencies might be fairly apparent to us and are probably the ones with which we have made pretty good progress. However, do you truly understand all the aspects of your heart? Have you ever rudely responded to someone and then silently asked yourself, "Where did that come from?" Sometimes we just can't believe what we've done or said. Perhaps areas of brokenness remain hidden to us in the deep recesses of our hearts. Because of lack of self-reflection, we may not even realize how corrupt parts of our character have become. On top of that, even if we are somewhat aware, most of us will actually want to repress such ugliness. Who likes to think ill of themselves? But these areas are where we are not conformed to the image of Christ and where the Spirit wants to perform His work.

The psalmist of old requested that God search His heart and reveal any "hurtful way" within him (Psalm 139:23-24). He then appealed to God to lead him in the "everlasting way." We need to make this prayer our own. Ask God to open our eyes to the hurtful ways inside us, where Christ has not yet been formed. Expect God to then confront us in some form or another. Perhaps through Scripture, a brother or sister, a book, or sermon, but whatever the means, we need this to occur for the Spirit to start probing our hearts. Never forget, character, good or bad, is part of who we are. As such, we may try to hold on and resist changes to some of these deeply-held traits.

Once we come to an understanding of our shortcomings, ask God's assistance in putting these old characteristics to death and help replace them with traits that are pure. Don't expect this to occur immediately. These old traits are intertwined with many aspects of our lives. We may want to consider seeking help from someone spiritual that we trust and would hold us accountable for making progress.

God's Word

Studying and reflecting on God's Word is critical for the pursuit of holiness for several reasons. First, our hearts need a regular dose of Scripture's penetrating power. As the writer of Hebrews states, God's Word has the ability to "judge the thoughts and intentions of the heart" (Hebrews 4:12). Power-packed to confront our shortcomings, God's Word pulls no punches. Unfortunately, we tend to neutralize its heart-revealing power by studying the Bible with the sole intent of increasing our knowledge. Without reflecting on how a particular passage personally speaks to our current life circumstances and character, our hearts are not likely to be impacted. Knowledge is great, but without mixing in some self-assessment at times, even studying God's Word can turn into a self-serving activity.

Second, God's Word reveals what holy character and conduct look like. Even though 2 Corinthians 3:18 indicates the Spirit is responsible for transforming us into the image of Christ, it also defines our role as "beholding." We "behold" God through reading of Jesus in the gospel (2 Corinthians 4:4-6). What rich soil we create when we let Jesus' life speak to us through the gospel story. Not in hard-cold facts, our Savior's character and actions are impressed upon us in story-form with real historical people.

Third, God's Word is the cornerstone of faith. Christ may dwell in our hearts because of the Spirit's power, but without our faith, His power is rendered useless (Ephesians 3:16-17). It was Paul's faith response to who Christ is and what He accomplished that allowed him to declare that "Christ lives in me" (Galatians 2:20). No longer did Paul pursue his own selfish desires, he now lived for the One who dwelt in his heart. But where does such faith come from? Faith's lifeblood is the Gospel of Christ (Romans 10:17). Faith developed devoid of serious contact with God's Word is destined to be corrupted by the world. Therefore, a holistic pursuit of holiness always includes our involvement with God's Word through various means.

Faithful Action

Paul makes it clear to Timothy that to be useful for service to God, one must be cleansed and sanctified (2 Timothy 2:20-26). He then explains that the sanctified life involves fleeing from youthful lusts and pursuing the virtues of righteousness, faith, love, and peace. Of course, Paul was addressing a specific situation affecting Timothy, but the general principle still applies to us. We must flee sinful lusts and pursue a virtuous lifestyle.

The metaphors of fleeing and pursuing are not just a call to passively change our inner character, but an appeal to dynamically act upon our new life orientation. Our pursuit of holiness takes place in the midst of other people. To get his point across, Paul provided Timothy with a few examples. Holy conduct produces fruitful conversations not constant bickering and strife. Holiness manifests itself in the gentle approach to teaching those who oppose us, keeping their best interests in mind. Holiness is acted out in the world, not behind closed doors of a church building.

Don't forget, have faith in the Spirit who is at work in you – you have a divine partner.

COOL DOWN

I would like for you to take a few minutes and make a list of all the things that encompass your Christian life – church activities, devotional time, ministering to others, praying, attending workshops, evangelism, and the like. Please include even little things; sending cards, phone calls, etc. Now honestly look at your list, and note how many of these activities are inward-focused versus outward-focused. Of all these activities, what percentage of them would you consider for your edification? What percentage is for serving others?

My experience tells me that serving others may be a little low on your totem pole. As usual, we humans kind of get things backwards. God's intention for creating us anew was to prepare us for performing good works (Ephesians 2:10). Our other activities should equip us to serve others (Ephesians 4:12). Jesus' earthly mission was all about serving (Matthew 20:28). The King of kings washing humanity's feet, going to the cross in our stead – what a servant, what a Savior!

Jesus had the heart of a servant, and with the goal of being transformed into His likeness, we should aspire to this quality as well. A lack of serving others is a surefire way to corrupt the image being formed in us. Living in a culture addicted to pursuing wealth, pleasure, and material possessions presents us with some tough challenges. Most of us have probably been more influenced by our self-serving culture than we would like to admit. We need to reverse this trend. A holy one, wholly serves.

Questions

1. How does the Holy Spirit work with you as a partner to help you pursue holiness?

2. Can you recall a recent incident when your behavior was inappropriate? What drove this behavior? Was the character trait that caused your conduct in line with Jesus'? What might you do to change it?

3. What excuses do people offer to defend their inappropriate behaviors?

4. Identify a few of Jesus' character traits by evaluating His interaction with others? Do you believe you embody these traits? If not, how might you make progress in bringing them about?

5. How might studying God's Word be self-serving? What can we do to change this? How does God's Word help in our pursuit of holiness?

6. How might the lack of serving corrupt the image of Christ being formed in us? What opportunities of service might you be neglecting?

Lesson 12
The Holy Church

Daily Readings:
Ephesians 2:20-22, 5:25-27; 1 Corinthians 3:16-17;
Hebrews 10:24-25; 2 Corinthians 6:16-7:1

WARM UP

Have you ever watched a game of "herd" soccer? If your children played soccer at an early age, you know exactly what I am talking about. Up and down the field, wherever the ball goes a herd of kids follow it. No one stays in their positions except the goalies, all the other kids just spastically kick and chase the ball around in a herd. On one occasion, I remember watching my five year-old son's soccer game. I noticed the goalie had become bored since all the action was taking place on the other end of the field. Intrigued by the goal's net, the goalie suddenly realized that his head might just fit into one of its holes. About the time he squeezed his little head through the hole, the ball squirted out of the herd on the other end of the field and headed straight toward his goal.

As about thirty heads in the crowd turned toward the distracted goalie, everyone stood aghast at what was about to transpire. With everyone now yelling at the goalie, he frantically struggled to pull his head back through the net, while a kid from the other team ran up and kicked the ball into the goal. Sometimes I believe we are like this fun-loving goalie. Wrapped up in our own little world, we neglect the very thing that God created to help us achieve our spiritual goals together – the church.

WORK OUT

When I started thinking about this lesson, it dawned on me that I could not recall any preacher, teacher, or elder ever referring to the church as holy. In Christian groups steeped in formality, hearing the phrase "the holy church" might not be uncommon, but in all my years of attending various congregations, this designation has not tickled my ears. There could be many reasons for this, but let's take a look at God's Word and see how the bride of Christ is portrayed.

A Beautiful Bride

In Ephesians 5:25-27, Paul used Christ's love for the church as an example of how a husband should love his wife. What a high standard Paul placed on us husbands. This was no fair-weather love; it was radical. Christ went to the cross for His beloved bride. Examining a husband's love from this regard would be an interesting study, but I want to take you in another direction.

Christ not only died for us individually, He died for us collectively. His sacrificial love for the church brought about its sanctification and cleansing. Paul's reference to "the washing of water" (vs. 26) may have served to compare the effectiveness of a Greek wedding custom and Christian baptism. Bathing in a "supposedly" sacred stream's water was thought to cleanse the Grecian bride from impurities prior to her wedding. But to Paul, only the water of baptism possesses the ability to cleanse. Collectively speaking, the church comes into contact with the death of Christ at baptism (Romans 6:4) which has true cleansing power. "The word" with which this occurs was none other than the Gospel itself which is involved in the sanctification of all believers (John 17:17).

Purified and set apart in God's holiness, Jesus prepared for Himself a beautiful bride. Morally glorious without "spot or wrinkle," Jesus wedded a "holy and blameless" bride. The moral to this love story is that Christ's bride is holy. Not conformed to the world's corrupted nature, Christians reside in a holy place, where holiness can be properly pursued.

A Holy Temple

Paul gave a dire warning to the Corinthians concerning destructive behavior in the church (1 Corinthians 3:16-17). First, he reminded them that they were God's temple, and that His Spirit dwelt among them. Unlike 1 Cor. 6:19, where Paul was speaking to individuals, the "you" in this passage is plural, indicating that he was addressing the entire church. From a Corinthian's perspective, can you imagine the impact of Paul's statement? While temples were places of beauty, sacred, and the abode of the gods, Paul pointed out that the true and living God actually dwelt in their house churches. We are formed into a holy temple of the Almighty - what a profound thought to process for these former pagan worshipers. What a profound thought for us as well.

Living in a holy community dictated that the Corinthians were to live holy lives. Since their divisive conduct (e.g. see 1 Corinthians 1:10-13) stood in stark contrast to holiness's unifying properties, Paul knew some of the Corinthians were in dire straits. So Paul sent a warning shot over their bow, and stated that behavior leading to the destruction of God's holy church would result in that individual's destruction. In summary, you might want to think twice before stirring up trouble in God's church.

Years ago, a friend confided in me of his desire to tear apart his church's eldership. From my perspective, these elders were aptly qualified, and such an action would be like hitting a hornet's nest with a baseball. Stinging mad, many church members would enter into bitter disputes with one another, possibly destroying this once peaceful congregation. Typically, I try to gently guide people to possible solutions for their given problems, but this demanded the utmost directness. In no uncertain terms, I told him that he needed to repent of devising this factious course of action and immediately separate himself from those who contributed to his recently-developed enmity.

God loves the local church and walks amongst His people (2 Corinthians 6:16). We need to powerfully grab onto that vision. He created the church to spiritually mature His people (Ephesians 4:14). Factious behavior belongs to the world. Unity is the church's beacon to enlighten a skeptical world that God truly sent Jesus to redeem humanity (John 17:21).

Togetherness

Thank goodness we are not alone in our pursuit of holiness. When certain situations arise, I sometimes find it extraordinarily difficult to exhibit holy behaviors. I thank God that He placed me in a group on the same spiritual journey, where shared experiences can bring hope and encouragement and prayers can attend to my shortcomings. Exploring God's Word together brings exciting perspectives as to the practical nature of its teachings. But only through Christ are we supported, joined, and formed together to become a holy temple, a dwelling place suitable for God's Spirit (Ephesians 2:20-22). Without letting Christ lead and pervade the formation of His church, sadly we will just become another group of do-gooders, not His holy church.

COOL DOWN

At this point, we could discuss a number of ways that the church contributes to an individual's holiness. Many of these are fairly apparent or have already been alluded to or discussed, so I would like to hone in on just one especially beneficial role the church plays in this regard. Assembling together might present us with a wonderful opportunity to worship our glorious God, but such occasions also serve as an excellent setting to motivate others to express their love through good deeds (Hebrews 10:24-25). Spring-boarding us into action, the church serves as a conduit to exercise our holy character while it is under development.

Church services and other activities provide excellent venues for making the congregation aware of various needs. Announcements, bulletins, and one-on-one conversations allow for the dissemination of important information concerning such matters, but the Hebrews' writer notes that we should also put some mental energy into how to "stimulate" fellow Christians to meet those needs. Obviously, all needs are not created equal. Some are relatively straightforward, such as taking food to the bereaved, while others may require someone with a particular skill or life experience. Understanding the need and finding the *right* person to meet it is crucial.

Don't be bashful, most Christians are more than willing to help out, they just need their eyes opened to the opportunities before them. However, many desire someone to go alongside them the first few times out of the chute. Several years ago, I was made aware of an elderly woman whose stairs leading up to her trailer's front door were old and rickety. Being the consummate un-handyman, this was not a job I wanted to tackle by myself. I knew a brother who could easily take care of this by himself, but he was going to want me by his side. After replacing the wooden staircase, the genuine appreciation of this needful woman warmed both our hearts.

Smiles and words of gratitude strongly reinforce our developing nature, but people are unpredictable, such responses may not come. So always take solace in knowing that smiles from heaven accompany all your good deeds.

Questions

1. How does Jesus view the church? What resulted from His extreme love for her?

2. Have you ever thought about the implications that the church you attend is a holy temple of God? What does this tell us about God? How does this impact you?

3. How do you believe God views divisive behavior? What should be your reaction when someone tries to lure you into factious conversations or behavior?

4. What are some ways the church contributes to the development of holiness within its members? How does the fellowship of others play a part? What specifically do you need to take more advantage of?

5. Identify an opportunity where a good work is needed? How might you motivate someone to accomplish it? How do good works develop holiness within us?

6. How does congregational holiness impact our evangelistic efforts?

Lesson 13
The Ultimate Expression of Holiness

Daily Readings:
**Romans 5:6-11; Romans 8:31-39; Philippians 2:3-4;
Luke 15:1-32; 1 John 4:8-10**

WARM UP

If you have ever looked at a planet-view image of Mars, you probably noticed an immense geological feature on its surface near the equator. Science fiction fans might imagine Luke Skywalker entering this cavernous rift in his speedy spaceship in an attempt to evade Darth Vader. We earth-dwellers are mighty proud of our Grand Canyon, but the red planet hosts the grandest of canyons in our Solar System. Called the *Valles Marineris*, this enormous valley is actually a system of canyons. It stretches over an expanse about equal to the distance across the United States (2500 miles). At its deepest point, the *Valles Marineris* is six to seven times deeper than our Grand Canyon (6.25 miles). Typically this immense valley is about 31 to 62 miles wide, but maxes out around 375 miles at its widest point.

Could you imagine being an astronaut stranded on the opposite side of this valley from your base-camp? Outside the use of a space-ship, there is physically no way to traverse this vast abyss. Spiritually, we encounter such a chasm when sin enters our life. With unholiness marring our souls, an immense separation occurs between us and our holy God. No amount of human ingenuity or good behavior can mend this rift. God must act to bridge this enormous divide.

WORK OUT

Donald W. McCullough, in his book *The Trivialization of God*, pro-poses that God's holiness finds its ultimate expression in redeeming love. I believe he was spot-on with that observation. God's capacity to love sets Him apart from all His creation. Let's conclude our explora-tion of holiness by studying this remarkable aspect of God and con-sider any ramifications it may have on our daily walk.

Love Revealed

My encounter with Christ while taking the Lord's Supper does not always reach the depths I desire, but on a number of occasions, taking this memorial meal has left me with tears streaming down my face. Visualizing the horrific scenes that surround the cross, a grave sorrow starts to overtake my heart. Battle-hardened fists of cruel Roman sol-diers strike my Savior's face. After being scourged, spat upon, and hu-miliated, the King of kings is mockingly coronated with a lowly crown of thorns. Roman hammers eerily ring out on Golgotha as spikes are driven through the Son of God's flesh. As the rugged cross is raised, Jesus' blood-drenched body comes into view while hate-mongers continue to ridicule Him. I can't help but ask, "Why?" With eyes closed, reflecting on this dire chain of events, the answer comes – my sins required my Lord's death – and the tears uncontrollably flow.

Paul at times pulls no punches. In Romans 5:6-11, he described humanity as ungodly, sinners, and enemies of God destined for His wrath. Let this sink in for a minute. Sin not only separates you from God; you are now His enemy. Why such strong language? Paul is emphasizing an important quality about God's nature; His holiness is the polar opposite of sin. Our participation in sin not only ruins a wonderful relationship, we even pass the point of indifference or dislike – we become enemies to His holiness.

But Paul also used another term to describe humanity – helpless (vs. 6). Sin pollutes our souls with a foul stench that we cannot remove and God cannot tolerate. Powerless to save ourselves, God intervened. Merciful as well as holy, God's love streamed out of heaven, sending His Son to save us from our helpless state. His life was destined to give life.

To demonstrate that "God is Love," John used the ultimate example of love as proof (1 John 4:8-10). Seeing His beloved image-bearers lost and corrupted by sin, God was moved to an extreme solution. Not acting in response to love extended toward Him, God acted on His own initiative out of His remarkable loving nature. He sent Jesus into a desperate world to die on a cross for our sins that we might live. God loves us so much that he sent his *only* Son to facilitate our forgiveness and restore holiness to those who accept His love. Even though we were enemies of holiness, we became targets of love. What a God, what a Savior!

Divinely Bonded

Many times in life, things we tend to value are taken from us. Our companies reduce our benefits, our sweethearts are swept off their feet by another, the government takes away more of our salary by raising taxes, and the list goes on. We virtually have no control over such twists of fate. But when God repairs the spiritual separation between Him and you, nothing external to that relationship can tear you apart from Him (Romans 8:35-39). Neither the government, a boss, nor your worst tormenter can separate you from God's love in Christ Jesus. No created thing possesses such power, not even a mighty angel or Satan himself can break your bonds of love with the Almighty. Only you control whether this relationship will stay intact, God will do and has done His part. We can place great confidence in God's love for us, knowing that in re-establishing our relationship with Him even His own Son was not spared (Romans 8:32).

Unfamiliar Love

In an old song by the J. Geils Band, the songwriter recollects his failed attempts at love and at one point states, "I've been through diamonds, I've been through minks, I've been through it all, Love stinks!" Our culture has largely lost the concept of biblical love. I remember wondering a few years ago how Jesus could command me to love another person. It takes time for love to develop, and some people are not very lovable. It just did not seem fair to *command* me to love someone. Affected by my culture, I understood love in the context of romance (such as between husband and wife) or relations (such as between friends), but God's Word has a third aspect of love – *agape*. I've always felt that Philippians 2:3-4 richly defines this biblical concept of love. With all humility, we are to selflessly look after the needs of others and sacrificially meet them as we can. Certainly *agape* contains a developmental dimension, but we can all start immediately applying it to our relationships.

God reached out to us with *agape* love by accomplishing what we could not do for ourselves. He sacrificially offered up the life of His Son for the forgiveness of our sins. As such, God can justly ask us to *agape* others, even enemies. Seeking the welfare of others is the holy approach to life. Seeking vengeance and wishing others ill will corrupt our hearts. Which do you believe our world practices?

COOL DOWN

A number of years ago, a remorseful young woman tearfully came forward during the invitation seeking forgiveness for an unspeakable sin. A short time later, the preacher told her that people were too quick to forgive her. Was this preacher justified in his comment considering the "magnitude" of the sin? Did he truly understand God's approach to repentant sinners?

Plagued by the grumbling of the Pharisees and scribes over His reception of sinners, Jesus shared three parables concerning God's response to the lost and wayward sinners (Luke 15:1-32). In the parables of the Lost Sheep and Lost Coin, Jesus portrayed God's concern for the lost in that He actively pursues them. But in the parable of the Prodigal Son, Jesus revealed an even more intimate side to His Father.

After squandering his inheritance on loose living (harlots, vs. 30), the prodigal found himself watching over swine and longing for their food. Not a great situation for a Jew who considered pigs as unclean. The prodigal recognized his sinful state and decided to return home and throw himself upon the mercy of his father. Next comes an amazing portrayal of God, the father was watching and caught a glimpse of his wayward son off in the distance. Running to him, the father hugged and kissed his disrespectful, harlot-chasing, and unclean young son.

What a wonderful, compassionate image of God. He is not chomping at the bit to lecture, punish, or publicly shun us. He longingly watches for our return, and when we again turn to Him, He rushes to love on us, honor us, and celebrate our homecoming. Our majestic, high and holy God hugging and kissing on me, what a shocking thought.

How do you love? Like the Father or like a Pharisee or the prodigal's brother? When someone turns his life back to God, do you love on them or shun them, holding on to hard feelings? To be holy like God, we need to love like God, and wholly love others.

Questions

1. What does the separation that sin causes between us and God teach us about God?

2. How do we know that God is love? How has God's love been revealed in your life?

3. How does Romans 8:35-39 relate to our eternal security and the "once-saved, always-saved" teaching?

4. Explain what *agape* love is? What examples of it have you seen in your life? Can you identify a couple opportunities where you could extend this love to others?

5. How do you feel about Jesus' portrayal of God in the parable of the Prodigal Son? Do you find it easy to be like God in this regard? What might stand in your way of expressing love to a penitent brother? How might you remove such hindrances?

6. If *agape* love is the outward expression of inner holiness, how would you rate your personal holiness? The holiness of your congregation? How would your community view your congregation's level of holiness?